FROM CELL PHONES TO VOIP

The Evolution of Communication Technology
Technology Books
Children's Reference & Nonfiction

Speedy Publishing LLC

40 E. Main St. #1156

Newark, DE 19711

www.speedypublishing.com

Copyright 2017

In this book, we're going to talk about the evolution of communication from the earliest phones to cell phones to VOIP. So, let's get right to it!

Before telephones were invented, there wasn't a way for anyone to speak to someone else and get a response unless they were in the same place. Today, cell phones and other communication technologies allow us to talk to anyone, anywhere. They are an integral part of our lives and we're communicating more than ever before.

Phones have changed a great deal from when they were first introduced in the late 1800s. In addition to looking a lot different, they are much easier to carry and use. They also have many additional functions we can use and are not just for speaking anymore!

Smartphones today can be used to:

⇒ Take pictures and put graphics with them

⇒ Send texts and emoticons

⇒ Surf the web

⇒ Find your location

⇒ Watch the weather forecast

⇒ Wake you up with an alarm in the morning

⇒ Play games

⇒ Learn something new

⇒ Watch videos

⇒ Pay bills

⇒ Play music

young couple watching videos

log in
Cooking Blog
Cheesy shortcakes
Fresh & Easy!!!
Carrot Cream
Spanish Octopus
Roasted Peppers
Desserts
Recipe list

If you have your own smartphone, you probably use it dozens of times every day and don't think about all the wonderful things it can do.

WHEN WAS THE TELEPHONE INVENTED?

Many different inventors had the idea for a telephone at approximately the same time. However, Alexander Graham Bell was able to get his patent filed before anyone else, so he is considered to be the official inventor of the telephone. Bell was initially trying to figure out how to send several messages at one time over a telegraph wire.

vintage telephone

telegraph

At that time, telegraphs were being used to send text messages across the country. While he was working on this invention, he realized that there might be a way to send the sound of a person's voice from one place to another, and that's how the idea for the telephone was born.

Eventually, Bell formed a company called the Bell Telephone Company to sell his new technology. Today, that company is still in existence and is called American Telephone and Telegraph, AT&T for short. AT&T is the largest telecommunications company in the world.

public telephone

ROTARY PHONES

The first phones were clunky boxes that were hung up on the wall. You had to speak to an operator to make a phone call to someone. A new form of the telephone was introduced in the early 1900s. This version still hung on the wall, but it was much smaller.

The technology had changed so that people could make phone calls person to person and didn't have to go through an operator. These types of phones were called rotary phones. To dial the phone number, you had to put your finger into a hole and rotate the circular piece for each number.

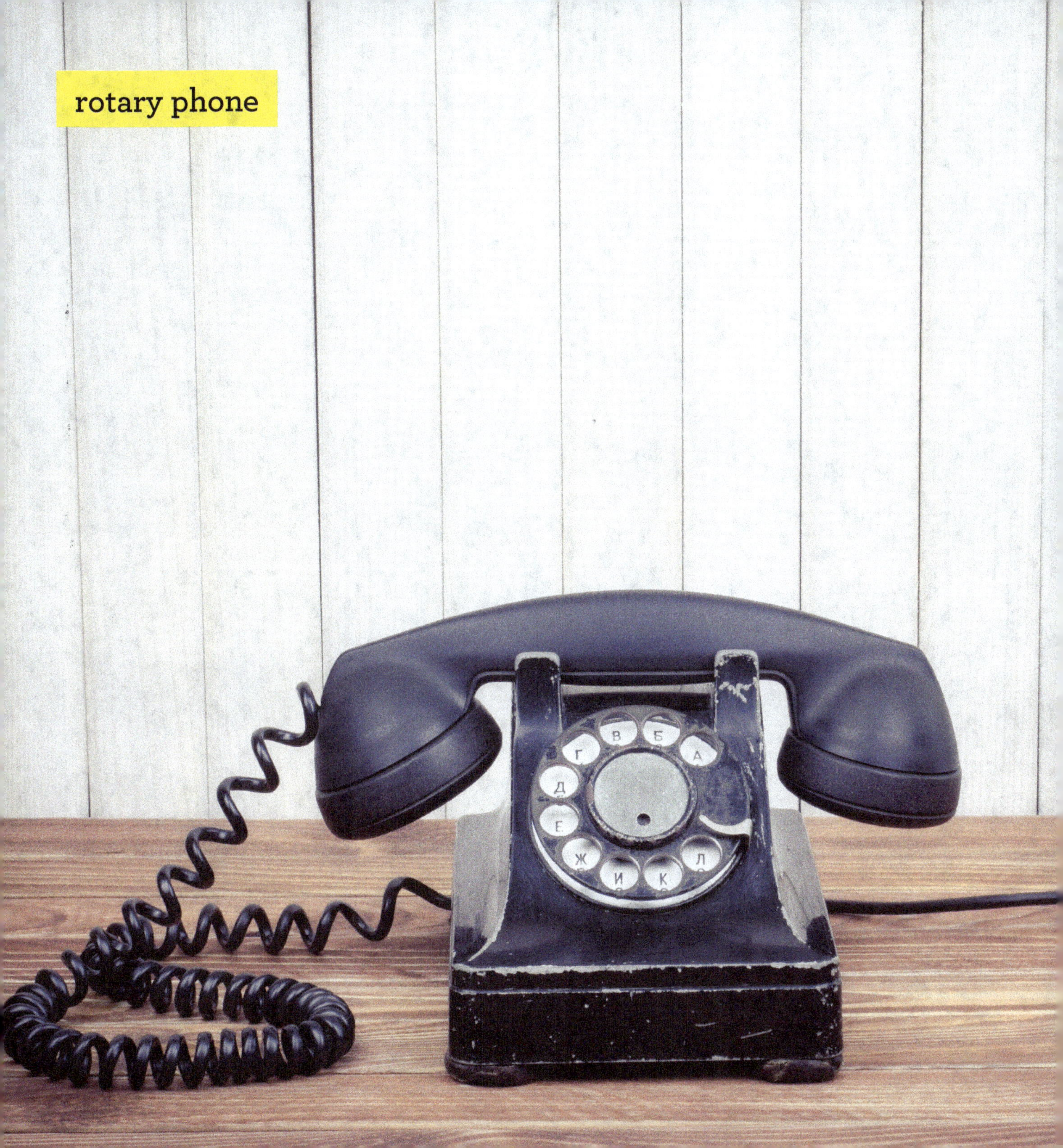
rotary phone

Soon, rotary phones evolved so that they could be placed on desks and tables. However, if you wanted to walk around with them, you needed a very long wire because they had to be connected to the wall. Rotary phones were popular through the 1970s. Today these phones are considered antiques.

TOUCH-TONE PHONES

Touch-tone phones became available in the early 1960s. However, most homes and businesses didn't have them until the 1980s. The reason is that they were much more expensive than rotary phones to produce and for consumers to buy. At the beginning, phone companies didn't make too many of them due to these factors. After a few years, the prices dropped. Then, people began switching from rotary phones to touch-tone phones because their buttons were much easier to push than using a rotary dial.

touch-tone phone

cellphone

CELLULAR TELEPHONES

Now that people could pick up a phone and move around with it, they started to think about phones that could work from anywhere in the world with no wires attached. Cellular phones were invented to serve that need. The very first phone call on a cellular phone was placed on April 3, 1973. Martin Cooper made the call. He was the general manager of the Communications Systems Division of Motorola and he called his rival on the phone!

The first cellular phones available for consumers, called cell phones for short, were available in the 1980s, but there was a problem with them. They were huge and very bulky. Most people that had them carried them inside their briefcases or stored them in their cars. They were used primarily for business as well as emergency calls. However, by the beginning of the 2000s, cell phones had changed dramatically.

As cell phones became smaller and easier to carry, they became much more accessible for the everyday consumer. Cell phones were now mobile phones and phone calls could be made from anywhere that had reception from cell phone towers. As time went on, cell phones got smaller, less heavy, and lost their bulky touch-tone key pads, which were replaced with digital key pads that came up on screen.

WHAT'S THE DIFFERENCE BETWEEN A CELL PHONE AND A SMART PHONE?

The difference between a cell phone and a smart phone is the types of functions that the phone provides. Both types of phones connect through communications networks that are wireless, either through radio waves or through satellite transmissions.

100%
9:99AM
Enter Passcode
1
2
3
4
5
6
7
8
9
0
Emergency
Cancel

Most cell phones allow people to talk to each other, send short messages, called SMS for Short Message Service, or send other kinds of media like photos or short video clips using Multimedia Message Service, called MMS. Some newer cell phones allow the user to surf the Web and answer e-mails.

In addition to cell phones, in the early 1990s, personal digital assistants were introduced. At the beginning, these personal digital assistants, PDAs for short, were developed to help people keep themselves organized. In general, they used a stylus, which is a form of pen, instead of a keyboard. At the beginning, these PDAs didn't have phone or fax services, but then evolved to include these functions too.

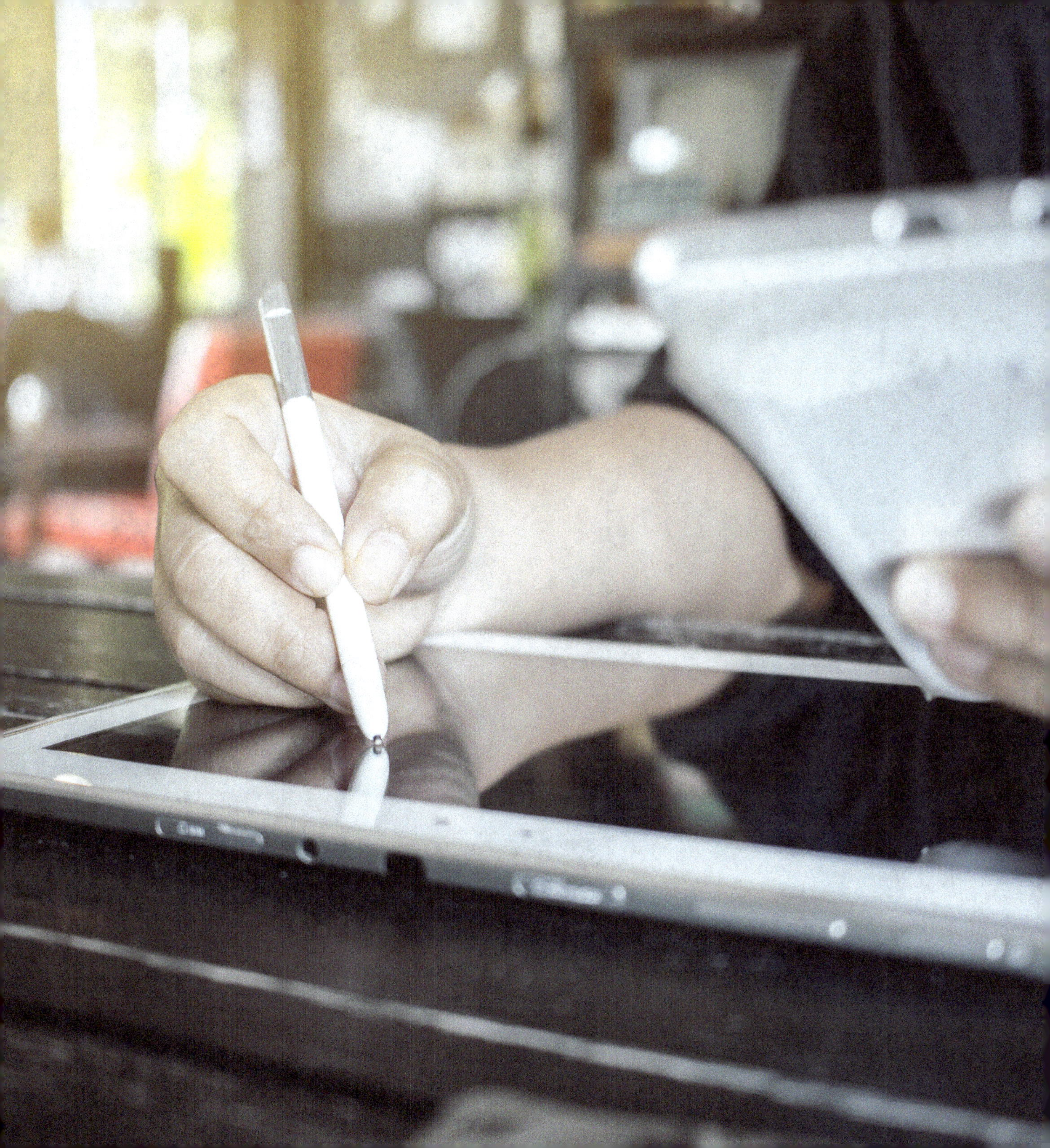

smartphone

For a while, people started to carry several different devices and it wasn't practical. The smartphone grew out of the need to combine the functions of a cell phone with the functions of a personal digital assistant. There's really no standard definition for a smartphone. Most phones that have more capabilities than standard cell phones are now considered smartphones.

There's also a category called PDA phones. These phones place more emphasis on their PDA capabilities than their cell phone capabilities. There are many different phones on the market and some of them are like small-size personal computers or PCs.

WORLD NEWS
BUSINESS
MEDICAL
SPORT
TECHNOLOGY

Here are just a few of the different types of phones available today:

⇒ The Apple iPhone, which is a combination of an iPod and a smartphone

⇒ The LG Prada, which is a cell phone with a screen that works by touch

⇒ The Palm Treo 700p, which is a PDA phone

⇒ The HP iPAQ Mobile Messenger, which is a Pocket Personal Computer

So, in summary:

⇒ A cell phone is more a phone than anything else

⇒ A smartphone is a combination of a cell phone and a PDA with an emphasis on the phone

⇒ A PDA phone is a combination of a PDA and a cell phone with an emphasis on the PDA

SMARTPHONES

The smartphone was the next evolution of the cell phone. Smartphones have touch screens and also a digital keyboard that shows up on screen for you to type a text or a digital phone keyboard for when you want to type the numbers in for a phone call.

Using a smartphone, you can talk to anyone at anytime as long as there's wireless service available. You can surf the web to do research, you can buy tickets to a concert, or you can play a game.

VOIP

VOIP is an acronym for voice over internet protocol. The most popular VOIP service today is Skype. It provides a way for users to speak over the internet by voice, by video, and with instant messaging. People starting using Skype in 2003.

It was bought out by eBay in 2005 for a price tag of $2.6 billion. Today, it provides a way for millions of people all over the world to communicate freely over the internet. Of all the available VOIP services it's the most popular and is constantly being improved.

4G LTE
100%
12:45
Mon Apr 25
What are you looking for?
76°F Clear
New York
United States

WHAT'S THE FUTURE FOR SMARTPHONES?

As smartphones evolve, they'll be able to access the internet faster and faster. There are smartphones in the works that will have artificial intelligence. They'll be able to tell from your tone of voice what type of mood you're in!

In addition to sensing your mood, the cell phone of the future might be able to take your blood pressure reading or measure the rate of your heart. It might even be able to project a hologram map when you're lost in an unknown city.

SUMMARY

Telephones have evolved from big, clunky boxes on the wall to small handheld devices that perform a huge amount of functions. Smartphones are becoming smarter with every passing year. In addition to allowing us to talk to anyone on Earth at any time as long as a wireless network is available, they offer us the ability to tap into the internet, take selfies, play games, and use apps. Now the world of communication is right at our fingertips!

Awesome! Now that you know more about the evolution of communication from the invention of the telephone to cell phones to VOIP, you can read more about the fascinating life of the inventor of the telephone in the Baby Professor book Hello? Is This Mr. Graham Bell?

4G LTE
100%
12:45
Mon Apr 25
What are you looking for?
76°F Clear
New York
United States
20MP
F2.0 WIDE

Visit

BABY PROFESSOR
EDUCATION KIDS

www.BabyProfessorBooks.com

to download Free Baby Professor eBooks
and view our catalog of new and exciting
Children's Books

www.ingramcontent.com/pod-product-compliance
Lightning Source LLC
Chambersburg PA
CBHW060129120726
48003CB00009B/2830